Spotlight on
Mexico

Bobbie Kalman and Niki Walker

Crabtree Publishing
crabtreebooks.com

Spotlight On My Country

Created by Bobbie Kalman

For Francine, who loves Mexico,
Your music is my inspiration. Thank you for your beautiful songs!

Crabtree Publishing

crabtreebooks.com 800-387-7650

In Canada: We acknowledge the financial support of the Government of Canada through the Canada Book Fund for our publishing activities.

Published in Canada
Crabtree Publishing
616 Welland Avenue
St. Catharines, Ontario
L2M 5V6

Published in the United States
Crabtree Publishing
347 Fifth Avenue
Suite 1402-145
New York, NY 10016

Editor-in-Chief: Bobbie Kalman
Writing team: Bobbie Kalman, Niki Walker, Robin Johnson
Editor: Robin Johnson
Photo research: Crystal Sikkens
Design: Bobbie Kalman, Katherine Kantor, Robert MacGregor (front cover)
Production manager: Candice Campbell
Prepress technician: Katherine Kantor

Hardcover 978-0-7787-3451-2
Paperback 978-0-7787-3477-2
Ebook (pdf) 978-0-7787-8945-1

Printed in the U.S.A./062025/CP20250616

Library and Archives Canada Cataloguing in Publication
Kalman, Bobbie, 1947-
Spotlight on Mexico / Bobbie Kalman and Niki Walker.

(Spotlight on my country)
Includes index.

ISBN 978-0-7787-3451-2 (bound).--
ISBN 978-0-7787-3477-2 (pbk.)

1. Mexico--Juvenile literature. I. Walker, Niki, 1972- II. Title. III. Series.

F1208.5.K375 2007 j972 C2007-906308-X

Illustrations:
Barbara Bedell: pages 11 (coyote), 13 (peppers), 29, 30 (all except blue and black fish and yellow goldfish)
Katherine Kantor: pages 4, 5, 10, 13 (top left and corn tortillas), 30 (blue and black fish)
Scott Mooney: back cover, pages 17 (top right), 18, 20 (top), 22
Bonna Rouse: pages 8, 13 (beans), 16, 17 (all exept top right), 20 (bottom)
Margaret Amy Salter: pages 11 (butterflies), 13 (squash and corn), 30 (yellow goldfish)

Photographs:
© BigStockPhoto.com: pages 7 (bottom right), 8, 10 (flower and spider), 26 (top), 27 (bottom left)
© Marc Crabtree: page 29 (bottom right)
© Dreamstime.com: back cover, pages 3, 12 (bottom right), 14
© iStockphoto.com: pages 6, 10 (Iguana on cactus), 11 (top right except isolated butterflies), 15 (bottom), 21 (top), 25 (right), 27 (top right), 30 (left)
© 2008 Jupiterimages Corporation: pages 16, 22, 27 (bottom right)
© Bobbie Kalman: pages 11 (top left), 23 (middle at left), 29 (bottom left), 30 (right), 31 (top right)
© ShutterStock.com: front cover, pages 1, 4, 5, 6 (top and bottom left), 9 (bottom), 11 (isolated butterflies and bottom), 12 (top and bottom left), 13, 18, 19, 23 (all except middle at left), 24, 25 (left), 26 (bottom), 29 (top right), 31 (top left and bottom)
Other images by Comstock, Corbis, Corel, and Photodisc

Library of Congress Cataloging-in-Publication Data
Kalman, Bobbie.
Spotlight on Mexico / Bobbie Kalman and Niki Walker.
p. cm. -- (Spotlight on my country)
Includes index.
ISBN-13: 978-0-7787-3451-2 (rlb)
ISBN-10: 0-7787-3451-X (rlb)
ISBN-13: 978-0-7787-3477-2 (pb)
ISBN-10: 0-7787-3477-3 (pb)
1. xico--Juvenile literature. I. Walker, Niki, 1972- II. Title. III. Series.
F1208.5.K352 2007
972--dc22 2007042628

Contents

Bienvenidos!

Bienvenidos! Bienvenidos means "welcome" in Spanish. Welcome to Mexico! Mexico is a **country**. A country has **borders**. Borders separate land into countries. A country has people. A country also has **laws**. Laws are rules that people must follow.

This map shows the country of Mexico. Which three countries share their borders with Mexico? Which country is north of Mexico? Which countries are south of Mexico?

Where in the world is Mexico?

Mexico is part of a **continent**. A continent is a huge area of land. There are seven continents on Earth. They are North America, South America, Europe, Asia, Africa, Australia and Oceania, and Antarctica. Look at the map below. To which continent does Mexico belong? Which continent is south of Mexico?

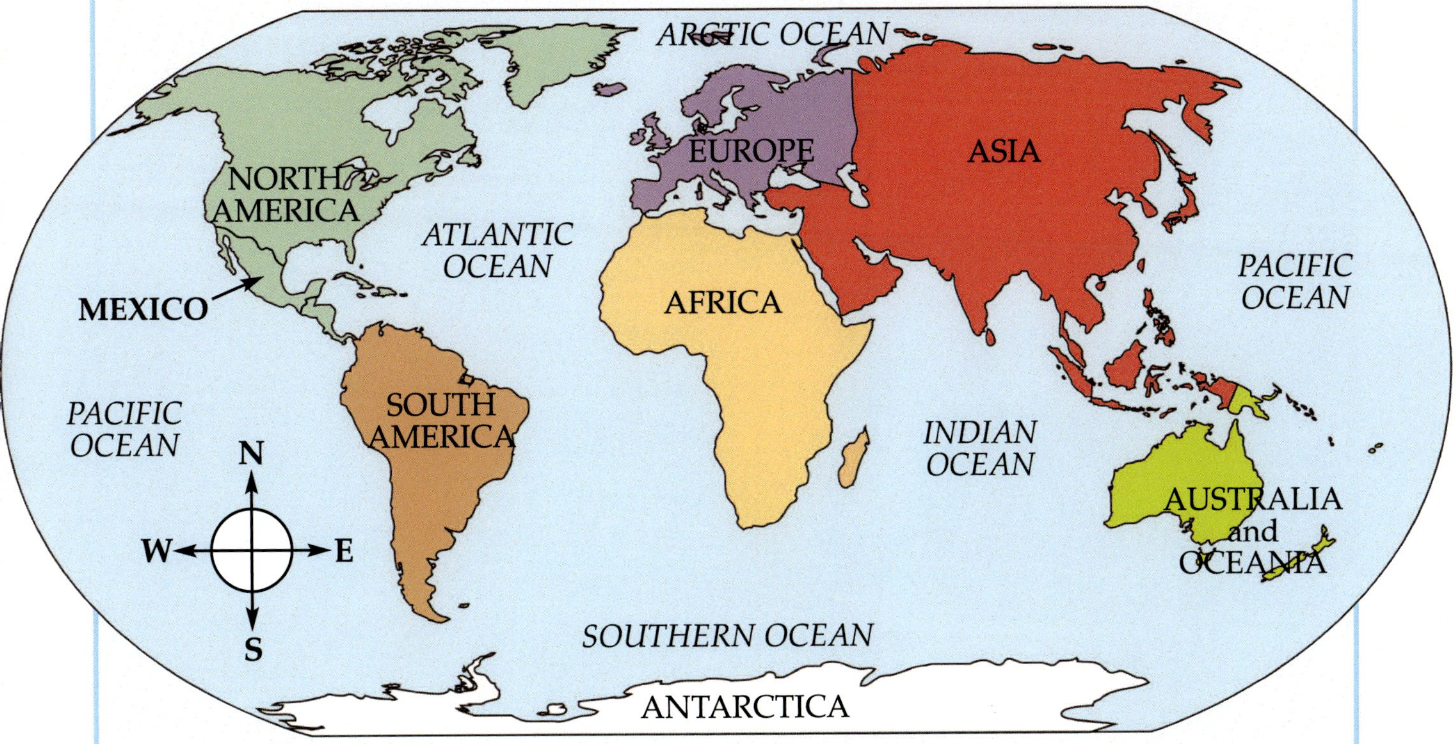

Mexico's people

The **population** of Mexico is over 108 million people. Population is the number of people who live in a country. People who live in Mexico are called Mexicans. Almost all Mexicans speak Spanish. It is the **national language**. Mexico has more Spanish-speaking people than any other country in the world! Do you speak Spanish? Some Spanish words are shown in the chart below.

This Mexican baby will soon speak Spanish.

Speak some Spanish!

Spanish	English
hola	hello
adiós	good-bye
por favor	please
gracias	thank you
sí	yes
no	no
Me llamo…	My name is…
¿Hablas español?	Do you speak Spanish?

Mexican families

Family is very important to Mexicans. Members of Mexican families take care of one another. Grandparents often live with their children and grandchildren. This grandmother lives with her son and grandchildren. She looks after her grandson while his parents work.

Mexico is a country of young people. One-third of Mexicans are under the age of 15! It is difficult for many parents to support their children. Some young people must quit school so they can work.

This mother and daughter are selling scarves on the street. Some Mexican children must work to help their families.

Other Mexican children have all the things they need and want.

Land and sea

The land in Mexico is not all the same. Mexico has **deserts**, mountains, **rain forests**, and beaches. The beaches are on the **coasts** of Mexico. A coast is land that is beside an ocean.

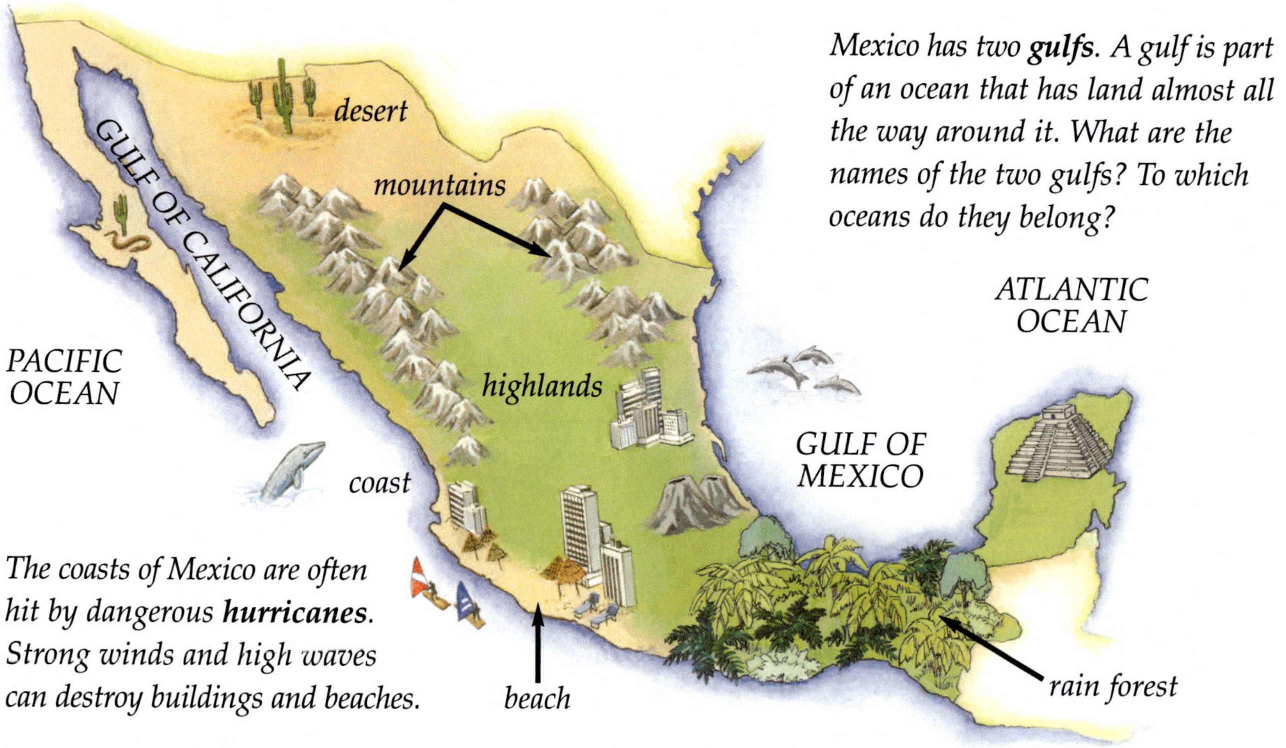

*Mexico has two **gulfs**. A gulf is part of an ocean that has land almost all the way around it. What are the names of the two gulfs? To which oceans do they belong?*

*The coasts of Mexico are often hit by dangerous **hurricanes**. Strong winds and high waves can destroy buildings and beaches.*

This hotel and beach in Mexico were damaged by a hurricane.

This picture shows a Mexican desert with mountains behind it. A desert is a hot area that gets very little rain. Few people live in this desert. In the mountains, the weather is cool year round.

Most Mexicans live in the ***highlands****. Highlands are areas of land that are on or around mountains. Highlands are good for farming. They have warm weather and many lakes and rivers.*

Rain forests are thick forests that receive a lot of rain. Many plants and animals live in ***tropical*** *rain forests in Mexico. Tropical rain forests are hot all year long.*

Plants and animals

The dahlia is Mexico's national flower. Dahlias grow in the highlands.

More than 200,000 **species**, or types, of plants and animals live in Mexico. The plants and animals live in different parts of the country. Each is suited to the area in which it lives.

Mexican red-kneed tarantulas are big, hairy spiders. They live in deserts in Mexico.

agave

Cactuses grow in Mexican deserts. Iguanas live in deserts, too. Both cactuses and iguanas need very little water. They are suited to living in these dry, hot areas.

prickly pear cactus

Parrots live in Mexico's rain forests. Many other animals also live there.

In winter, monarch butterflies live in Mexico. They fly long distances to forests that are found only on Mexico's mountains.

Coyotes live on the mountains of Mexico.

Dolphins live in the oceans around Mexico.

Villages and farms

Some Mexican people live in **villages**, or small towns. There are many villages and towns in Mexico's countryside. Most have houses, a church, a school, a market, and a **plaza**. A plaza is a public place where people meet.

*These **sombreros**, or large cowboy hats, are for sale at a market.*

*Many Mexicans go to churches such as this one. **Religion** is an important part of their lives.*

Mexican homes are colorful.

Many Mexicans are farmers. Farmers in Mexico grow corn, squash, beans, peppers, rice, wheat, bananas, coffee, and vanilla. Corn is the most important **crop**. Mexicans use corn to make many of the foods they eat (see pages 28-29).

bean plants

corn

squash

peppers

beans

This Mexican cowboy takes care of horses on a ***ranch****. A ranch is a large farm.*

Mexico's cities

Most Mexicans live in cities. Mexico's cities are busy places. They have many shops, museums, theaters, and art galleries. The biggest city in Mexico is Mexico City. It is the **capital** of the country. Mexico City is also the largest city in North America.

Mexico City has many beautiful old buildings. This building is called the Palace of Fine Arts.

A lot of people!

More than 20 million people live in Mexico City! Each year, many **tourists** visit this city, as well. The streets of Mexico City are crowded with cars and people. These people are walking in one of Mexico City's many parks.

Cabo San Lucas is a small city that is very popular with tourists. Cabo has beaches with big, beautiful hotels.

The government

The Mexican **government** is located in Mexico City. A government is a group of people who are in charge of a country or part of a country. The government makes important decisions and laws that people must follow. The Mexican **president** is the head of the government. The president and some members of his government work in the National Palace, shown above. The area in front of the palace is a square called El Zócalo.

The government of Mexico is a **federal republic**. In a federal republic, the citizens of the country **elect**, or choose, their leader. The people of Mexico elect a new president every six years.

*Mexicans **vote** to elect their president.*

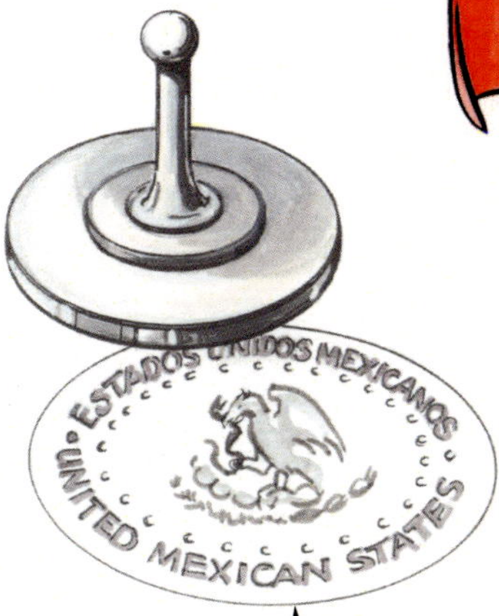

*Mexico's full name is the United Mexican States. The country is made up of 31 **states**.*

*Mexico's flag has green, white, and red stripes. The green stripe stands for **independence**, or freedom. The white stripe stands for religion. The red stripe stands for **unity**, or togetherness.*

Mexico's coat of arms

Mexico's **coat of arms** is in the middle of its flag. A coat of arms is a picture that stands for a country. Mexico's coat of arms shows a golden eagle with a snake in its beak. The eagle is standing on a cactus. A Mexican story tells that an eagle showed people of long ago where to build their city.

The first peoples

Thousands of years ago, Mexico was very different than it is today. Groups of native peoples lived on the land. The native peoples grew crops. They studied math and the stars. They built huge stone palaces, **pyramids**, and other buildings. The Olmecs, the Maya, and the Aztecs were great **civilizations** in Mexico. Civilizations are groups of people who create works of art and **record**, or write down, their histories.

*The Maya built huge cities. This picture shows part of an **ancient**, or very old, Mayan city called Palenque. Palenque contains beautiful buildings and artwork.*

The Aztecs were a very powerful native group. They built a large city, called Tenochtitlán. The Aztecs fought other native groups and became very rich. They ruled many people.

The Aztecs created a calendar, shown on the right. This calendar divided the year into 365 days.

The Olmecs were one of the earliest native groups to live in Mexico. They built huge statues of heads. They created many other kinds of art, as well.

Spanish rule

In 1519, a Spanish explorer named Hernán Cortés and his soldiers came to Mexico. Cortés wanted the riches and power of the Aztecs. The Spaniards fought the Aztecs and destroyed their city. They built Mexico City in its place. Mexico became a **colony** of Spain. A colony is an area that is ruled by a faraway country. Spain was a country across the ocean in Europe.

Moctezuma, the Aztec ruler, was friendly to Cortés and his soldiers when they arrived in Tenochtitlán. The Spanish later defeated the Aztecs in battle and destroyed their civilization.

The Spanish **colonists** treated the native Mexicans badly. The colonists took land, gold, and other things that belonged to the Mexican people. They made the native Mexicans speak Spanish. They forced the Mexicans to change their ways of life and become **Christians**. The Spaniards also brought **diseases**, or illnesses, that were new to Mexico. Many Mexicans died from these new diseases.

*Spanish colonists built **missions**, or places where Mexicans were taught how to be Christians.*

The Spanish people built Spanish-style homes, churches, and other buildings. The buildings had arches, fancy decorations, and tall spikes. They looked very different from the old Mexican buildings.

Revolution!

Most Mexicans did not want to be ruled by Spain. They wanted the freedom to rule themselves. In 1810, a priest named Father Hidalgo led the first **revolution** against Spain. A revolution is a war against a government. The Mexicans fought several revolutions. They won **independence** from Spain in 1821. Mexicans celebrate their independence each year. September 16 is Independence Day in Mexico.

(left) The Angel of Independence Monument in Mexico City was built to remember and celebrate Mexico's first revolution.

People call Father Hidalgo "the father of modern Mexico." He started the fight for Mexico's freedom.

Today, most Mexicans have both Spanish and native backgrounds. They are called **mestizos**. Native Mexicans still practice **traditional** ways and speak native languages.

The people shown here may look different, but they are all Mexicans!

This Maya woman is sewing beautiful handkerchiefs.

Mexican culture

Mariachi *bands wander through towns, singing songs and playing music.*

Mexican **culture** is a mix of old and modern ways. Culture includes art, music, history, clothing, food, and sports. Mexican culture is colorful and lively. It is filled with music, dancing, and a lot of fun.

This Mexican artist is making pots and plates. He will paint them in bright colors.

This woman is showing her riding skills in a traditional cowboy show called a ***charreada****.*

Fútbol, *or soccer, is the country's most popular sport. People in Mexico love to play and watch soccer. These young Mexicans are balancing soccer balls on their heads.*

Mexicans also enjoy **Lucha Libre**, *or masked wrestling. The wrestlers in Lucha Libre are called* **luchadors**. *Luchadors never take off their masks, so people do not know who they are. The picture on the left shows a luchador. The picture above right shows the kinds of masks that luchadors wear. The masks of the luchadors look like the masks of long ago, such as this ancient Aztec mask.*

Fiesta!

A **fiesta** is a party or celebration. Fiestas are fun times with family and friends. There is music, dancing, games, fireworks, and a lot of food! Mexicans have fiestas to celebrate birthdays, weddings, and other special occasions.

People often dress in costumes during fiestas. These costumed dancers are performing at a Mexican fiesta.

***Navidad**, or Christmas, is a long and happy holiday in Mexico. Mexicans have colorful parades called **posadas** for nine nights before Christmas Day. After each parade, children use sticks to try to break open **piñatas**. A piñata is a paper container filled with candy and small toys. The girl on the right is sad that her piñata will soon be broken.*

Day of the Dead

November 2 is the Day of the Dead. On this day, families decorate the graves of loved ones with candles and flowers. They are not sad, however. Mexicans believe that death is the beginning of new life. They have fiestas and celebrate the lives of those who have died. The Day of the Dead is like Halloween. There are funny skeletons everywhere!

Many Mexican fiestas end with colorful fireworks that light up the night sky.

Mexican foods

Food is an important part of Mexican culture. Traditional Mexican dishes are made with corn, beans, and **chilies**. Chilies are hot peppers. They are shown on the left. Have you eaten the Mexican dishes shown on these pages? Which Mexican meals would you like to try?

Cooking with corn

Corn is an important part of Mexican cooking. People usually make it into thin, round sheets called **tortillas**. Tortillas can be eaten plain like bread, or they can be fried to make chips and **tacos**. This taco looks delicious! It is easy to make. You can make tacos with ground beef, tomatoes, lettuce, and some grated cheese. Ask an adult to help you make one.

Salsa is a popular sauce. It contains chopped tomatoes, onions, parsley, and chilies. It is made with lemon or lime juice. You can eat your salsa with tortilla chips.

This salsa has some **guacamole** in it, as well. Guacamole is a dip made of mashed avocados.

Fajitas are wraps that are fun to make and eat, too. To make fajitas, you can use chicken strips, vegetables, salsa, guacamole, sour cream, and soft tortillas. Get creative and make one today!

Postcards from Mexico

Millions of tourists visit Mexico each year. Many come for the beautiful beaches and clear blue waters. Others enjoy exploring the **ruins** of ancient civilizations. Some visit Mexico for the culture, the food, and the fiestas! How would you spend your time in Mexico?

Many people go snorkeling in the colorful waters of the Gulf of Mexico.

The best part of Mexico is the friendly people that live there.

Xochimilco is known as the Floating Gardens. It is a place of many ***canals****. People can travel down the canals in colorful boats called* ***trajineras****.*

These dancers are performing the Mexican Hat Dance for tourists. It is the national dance of Mexico.

There are many ***volcanoes*** *to explore in Mexico. A volcano is a mountain that sometimes shoots out hot liquid rock called* ***lava****. The large volcano in this picture is called Popocatépetl. Its name means "smoking mountain" in the Aztec language. How do you think it got its name?*

Glossary

Note: Some boldfaced words are defined where they appear in the book.

canal A narrow, human-made waterway through which boats travel

capital The city in which a country's government is located

Christian A person who follows the teachings of Jesus Christ

colonist A person who lives in a colony

crop Plants grown by people for food

hurricane A big storm with fast-moving winds, which bring heavy rains

independence Freedom to rule one's own country

national language The language that is spoken by most people in a country

pyramid A large stone building that is shaped like a triangle

religion A set of beliefs about God or gods

ruins Parts of buildings that remain after a civilization has been destroyed

state A part of a country that has its own people, leaders, and rules

tourist A person who travels to a place for fun

traditional Describing ways that have been practiced for many years

tropical Describing an area that has hot, wet weather

vote To choose one person from a list of people

Index

Red kangaroos live in the outback. They can go for long periods of time without water.

Sturt's desert pea is one of Australia's best-known wildflowers. It grows in the outback.

Uluru

Rock formations

Australia has many large rock formations. A rock formation is a rock with an unusual shape. The most famous rock in Australia is Uluru, shown above. It is one of the largest rocks on Earth. Uluru is found in the Simpson Desert in the outback.

Wild and amazing

Australia has thousands of kinds of plants that are not found anywhere else on Earth. There are trees, flowers, and other plants that are truly different and amazing. Australia's animals are also unusual. Some of the wild animals that live in Australia do not live in other countries.

Huge eucalyptus trees grow in Australia. Koalas climb these tall trees and eat the leaves that grow on them. Koalas eat a lot of leaves!

This flower is called a kangaroo paw. It grows only in parts of Western Australia.

Marsupials and monotremes

Australia has many animals called **marsupials**. Marsupials are **mammals**. Most marsupial mothers feed and carry their babies in pouches on their bodies. Kangaroos and koalas are marsupials with pouches. Other unusual animals are **monotremes**. Monotremes are mammals that lay eggs instead of giving birth. Echidnas and platypuses are monotremes.

An echidna mother lays an egg into a pouch on her body. After the egg hatches, the baby drinks its mother's milk inside the pouch.

A Tasmanian devil is a marsupial that lives in Tasmania. It is about the size of a small dog.

A quokka is a small marsupial. It is about the size of a cat. There are not many quokkas left on Earth.

*A duck-billed platypus is a monotreme that looks like a duck. It lays eggs inside a **burrow**, or hole.*

Who are Australians?

This boy is an Australian Aboriginal.

There are more than 20 million people in Australia. People who live in Australia are called Australians. The first Australians were **Aboriginals**, or native peoples. Today, most Australians have English, Irish, or Scottish **ancestors**. Most speak English.

This Australian is part Asian.

This child's ancestors are Irish.

These girls are Chinese Australians.

G'day mate!

"G'day mate!" is how Australians greet their friends. Australians are very friendly! They welcome people from all over the world to their country. People from Europe, Asia, Africa, North America, and South America have come to live in Australia.

This child's face is painted like an Australian flag. You do not have to wear a flag to be an Australian!

These people may not look the same, but they are all Australians!

The first peoples

Aboriginals first came to Australia from Asia about 60,000 years ago. More than 400 groups of Aboriginals lived in Australia. Some groups were **nomadic**. Nomadic peoples travel from place to place in search of food and water. Some Aboriginals who lived near the coasts were not nomadic. They found food in one place and lived there.

Torres Strait Islanders

Another group of people came to Australia about 12,000 years ago. These people came from New Guinea. They **settled** on the islands off the northeast coast of Australia. These Australians are known as the Torres Strait Islanders.

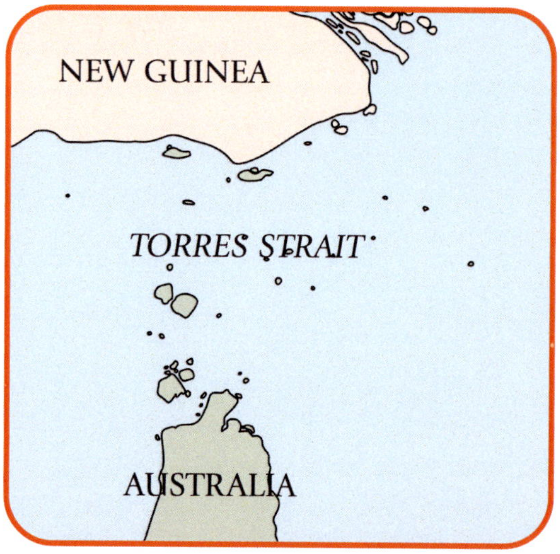

Practicing traditions

Today, most Aboriginals live in cities and towns. Some still live the way Aboriginals lived long ago, however. They travel from place to place and practice their **traditions**. Traditions are ways and beliefs that have been practiced for many years. Some of the traditions are passed down through ceremonies such as **corroborees**. Corroborees are for celebrating important events in life and for giving thanks.

The man above is talking about the Dreaming. The Dreaming consists of stories from long ago, in the time of the first ancestors. It tells how the land, animals, and people were created.

During corroborees, people paint their bodies with patterns that were used long ago.

Boomerangs were once used by Aboriginals for hunting. Today, they are used in sporting events.

People from Europe

These English prisoners are being loaded onto a ship that will take them to Australia.

People from Europe sailed to Australia in the 1600s, but they did not stay. Years later, an explorer named James Cook claimed Australia as an English **colony**. At that time, England had many prisoners and not enough jails. It began using Australia as a **penal colony**, or a great big jail. The first ship filled with prisoners and prison guards arrived in Australia in 1788. The prisoners were forced to build bridges and buildings and to plant **crops**. Crops are plants grown to be used by people.

Port Arthur is a prison in Tasmania. It was once used to hold England's most dangerous prisoners.

Free settlers

In the 1830s, people from England, Ireland, Scotland, and Germany came to live in Australia. They were not prisoners. They were free **settlers**. A settler is a person who lives in an area where there are not many people. Many of the settlers became **squatters**. Squatters take over land that they do not own. Many Aboriginals were killed trying to keep the squatters off native lands.

Thousands of free settlers sailed to Australia to start new lives. They traveled on big ships.

England sent explorers Robert Burke and William Wills to Australia to find new land for settlers. The explorers were not prepared for the heat of the outback. They died in the desert.

Caroline Chisholm helped women who came to Australia on their own. She found them places to live and trained them for jobs.

The government

Australia is a **commonwealth**. A commonwealth is a country that has its own government but is also connected with another country. The Queen of England is Australia's queen, but she does not rule Australia. Australia's government makes the decisions for its people. The **Prime Minister** is the head of the Australian government.

The blue color, the big star, and the Union Flag on Australia's flag all stand for Great Britain.

January 26 is Australia Day. It is one of the biggest holidays of the year. On this day, Australians celebrate their country and its people.

Australia is a democracy

Australia is a **democracy**. In a democracy, people choose their government leaders by **voting** for them. Australia's leaders are **elected**, or chosen, by the people of Australia. Australia's federal government is a **parliament**. It is made up of two government **houses**, or groups. They are the Senate and the House of Representatives.

Australians vote for their leaders. To vote is to choose one person from a list of people.

Australia's federal government meets in the Parliament House in Canberra. Canberra is the capital of Australia.

The House of Representatives meets in this room of the Parliament House.

Australia's cities

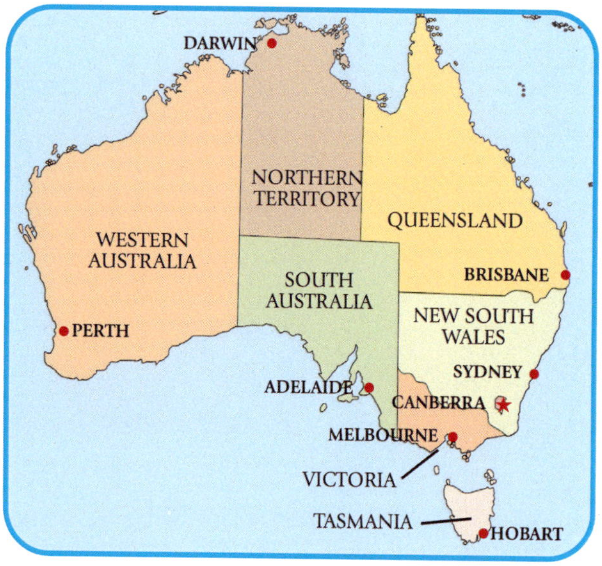

Australia's most important cities are shown on this map. They are the capital cities.

Most Australians live in cities. Australia's big cities are found on the coasts, where the weather is mild. Sydney is the largest and oldest city in Australia. Some of the other cities in Australia are Melbourne, Perth, Brisbane, Adelaide, and Hobart. Canberra is a small **inland** city. Inland means it is not on a coast.

Brisbane is the third-largest city in Australia. The Brisbane River divides the city.

Melbourne is the second-largest city in Australia. It is called the Garden City. It has many parks.

Hobart is Tasmania's largest city. Behind Hobart is Mount Wellington.

(right) The most famous building in Australia is the Sydney Opera House. Its roof was built to look like the sails of a ship.

*(below) Perth is on the west coast of Australia. It is far from any other city. Perth is **isolated**, or on its own.*

Farming and fishing

Grapes grown in Australia are made into red and white wines. The wines are sold in countries all over the world.

Most of Australia's land is too hot and dry for farming. People still grow many kinds of crops, however. Farmers in Australia grow grains such as wheat, rye, and barley. Different fruits and vegetables, as well as sugar cane and peanuts, are also grown. On Australian **ranches**, or large farms, animals such as sheep and **cattle** are raised. Both the farm animals and the crops were brought to Australia from Europe long ago.

Rapeseed, or canola, grows in Australia. Canola oil comes from the seeds of these yellow flowers.

There are ten times as many sheep in Australia as there are people! Sheep are raised on huge ranches called ***stations****. The sheep are raised for their meat and wool. Australia* ***produces****, or makes, more wool than any other country does. The wool is called Merino wool.*

Cattle are also raised on stations. They are raised for their beef. Much of Australia's beef is sold to other countries.

Australians catch all kinds of fish in the oceans and seas. They also trap lobster and shrimp.

Hamburgers, french fries, and onion rings are favorite foods in Australia. Fish and chips are also very popular.

Australians often cook their seafood on barbecues. These shrimp are cooking on the "barbie."

Outdoor fun

These students are on a school trip. They are visiting a lighthouse.

Australians spend a lot of time outdoors. The weather is usually warm, and most people live near coasts. There are many ways to have fun in Australia. Which of these Australian outdoor activities would you like to try?

These children are going for a camel ride. There are many camels in Australia's outback.

This young boy is hiking in a grassy area called "the bush." Will he see a wallaby there? A wallaby is a small marsupial.

Australians spend a lot of time at the beach. They even go on Christmas Day! In Australia, Christmas is in summer.

This girl is decorating a Christmas tree made of sticks on a quiet beach.

Many people surf in Australia's huge waves.

Tubing is also fun!

In surfboat rowing races, people race to a spot in the ocean and then back again. The waves are rough!

Your works of art

Aboriginal art is very colorful. It is also fun to make! Artists use a lot of dots and **geometric** shapes. You can make your own works of art. Use the pictures on these pages to get started.

Aboriginals painted pictures of animals on tree bark. They used dots, stripes, triangles, diamonds, circles, squares, ovals, and zigzags to create their art. Find these shapes in the lizard, turtle, and kangaroo pictures on this page. Then use the shapes to make your own works of art. Have fun!

Use dots to make a simple design, such as the one above, or a picture of an animal, such as the turtle below. Use brightly colored dots to create your pictures.

This kangaroo was painted on tree bark. It has many lines and shapes. You can make a picture like this, too. Hop to it!

Glossary

Note: Some boldfaced words are defined where they appear in the book.

Aboriginal A person who is first to live in an area

ancestor Someone who lived long ago and from whom another is descended

capital The city in which the government of a country, state, or territory is located

cattle Cows and oxen that people raise for their meat, milk, or hides

colony An area ruled by a country that is far away

commonwealth An area with its own government, but which is connected with another country, such as England

coral reef An area of the ocean that is made up of the coverings of live coral polyps and the skeletons of dead corals

desert A hot, dry area of land

geometric Made up of simple lines and shapes, such as circles and triangles

harbor An area of water near a coast where boats are protected from wind and waves

mammal An animal that is born, has hair or fur, and drinks its mother's milk

marsupial A mammal that grows in its mother's pouch after it is born and drinks its mother's milk there

monotreme A mammal that hatches from an egg and drinks mother's milk

outback A hot, dry desert area of Australia, where very few people live

parliament A government that is made up of elected and non-elected members

rain forest A forest that gets a lot of rain for part of the year or all of the year

scuba dive To swim under water while wearing a tank of air

settle To make a home and live in a place where few other people live

swamp An area of wet land that has trees, bushes, and other plants growing in it

valley A low area of land with mountains or hills around it

Index